The Lord is My Shepherd

This book belongs to:

"The Lord is my shepherd;
I shall not want."

The Lord is my loving shepherd.
He gives me what I need.

"He maketh me to lie down in green pastures;"

He blesses me with
a place to rest.

"He leadeth me beside the still waters."

He gives me peace.

"He restoreth my soul;"

He gives strength to my spirit.

"He leadeth me in paths of righteousness for his name's sake."

He helps me do what is right, so that others will see how good the Lord is.

"Yea, though I walk through the valley of the shadow of death,"

So, even when things look
dark and scary ...

"I will fear no evil;
for thou art with me;"

I will not be afraid,
because God is with me.

"Thy rod and thy staff, they comfort me."

He protects me and brings me comfort.

"Thou preparest a table before me in the presence of mine enemies;"

He blesses me even in front of those who don't like me.

"Thou anointest my head with oil; my cup runneth over."

God welcomes me with his love.
I overflow with his blessings.

"Surely goodness and mercy shall follow me all the days of my life;"

His goodness and love will always be there for me.

"And I will dwell in the house of the Lord forever."

And I will live with him forever,
here and in heaven.

Find the matching pair of sheep

Follow the dots to finish the picture

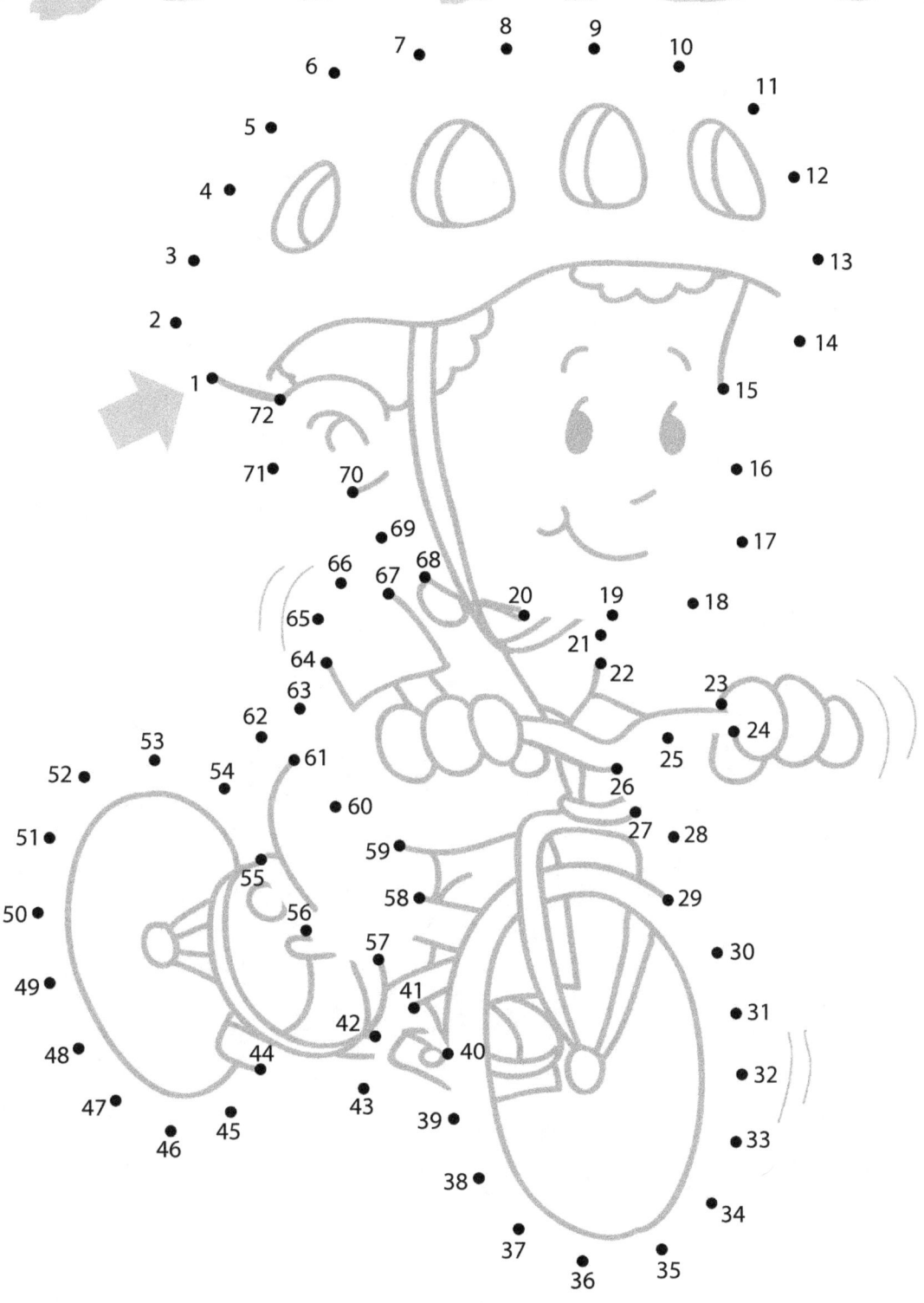

Go through the sheep maze

Match the shapes in the box, to the picture

Find the 7 differences.

Draw a picture in each frame of how God take care of you.

iCHARACTER

Published by iCharacter Ltd. (Ireland)
www.icharacter.org
By Agnes and Salem de Bezenac
Illustrated by Agnes de Bezenac
Copyright. All rights reserved.
All Bible verses adapted from the KJV.

Copyright © 2012. All rights reserved. No part of this book may be reproduced in any form or by any electronic or mechanical means, including information storage and retrieval systems, without written permission from the publisher or author, except in the case of a reviewer, who may quote brief passages embodied in critical articles or in a review.

www.ingramcontent.com/pod-product-compliance
Lightning Source LLC
Chambersburg PA
CBHW081432070526
44586CB00020B/2565